Letters f

MW01142008

Barry Dempster

Letters from a Long Illness with the World

... the D. H. Lawrence Poems

Brick Books

Canadian Cataloguing in Publication Data

Dempster, Barry, 1952-
  Letters from a long illness with the world:
  the D.H. Lawrence Poems

Poems.
ISBN 0-919626-64-5

  1. Lawrence, D. H. (David Herbert), 1885-1930 - Poetry.
  I. Title.

PS8557.E4827L4 1993   C811'.54   C93-093958-1
PR9199.E4827L4 1993

The support of the Canada Council and the Ontario
Arts Council is gratefully acknowledged. The support
of the Government of Ontario through the Ministry of
Culture, Tourism and Recreation is also gratefully
acknowledged.

Cover art 'Liberation' by F.H. Varley, collection of the
Art Gallery of Ontario (Gift of John B. Ridley, 1977,
and donated by the Ontario Heritage Foundation, 1988)
and the F.H. Varley Estate/Mrs. D. McKay. Cover
design is by Karen Ruttan.

Typeset in Trump Mediaeval, printed and bound by
The Porcupine's Quill. The stock is acid-free Zephyr
Antique laid.

Brick Books
Box 38, Station B
London, Ontario
N6A 4V3

For Karen

Contents

Lawrence knew that identity meant nothing; the important thing was entity, pure being.

… Anthony Burgess

Fade far away, dissolve, and quite forget
  What thou among the leaves hast never known,
The weariness, the fever, and the fret.

… John Keats

My God, but I can only say
I touch, I feel the unknown!
I am the first comer!
Cortes, Pisarro, Columbus, Cabot, they are nothing, nothing!
I am the first comer!
I am the discoverer!
I have found the other world!

... D.H. Lawrence

Green as the Vein in a Young Man's Desire...
Eastwood 1906

Green as a leaf's vein. Green as
a thumbprint in moss. Green
as confetti on stillborn ponds
as infant grass.
Asleep in a meadow
my bare chest stains green.
The nestled loin stone
the polished jade.

Somehow the forest overwhelms
most of life. Chestnut roots
crack kitchen floors, holly leaves
scratch downstairs doors, rabbits
eat entire dresser drawers.
I dive from my gaping bedroom window
and am instantly stripped and shrunk.

The mines grow arthritic, blacken
back to dirt and undergrowth. The town
squats on its squalid hill and strains.
In the moonlight a young man
runs tiny in the valley; a darting
nakedness, escape. In a bed
of violets, an exhausted embrace.

Women here turn red as berries
their slippers sinking in the leaves.
Shopgirl smiles whisked aside, strands
of scented hair. Bare ankles
marvellous in blue brooks. I would like
nothing better than to bleed
those berries between my fingertips.

Such are the tripping fantasies
of an Eastwood lad with the woods
set free in his nerves and wrists.
If only the world were totally green.
Men walking entire countries
with nothing hidden, blossoms
bursting in their eyes, each glance
a colour, a bouquet of flesh.

Green as the vein in a young man's
desire. May all the lovers in the world
be smudged with fingerprints.
The forest thrives through my
bedroom window and carries me away.
Even my nipples are hard as jade.
The world sharpened to a blade of grass.

… much thought to the scheme of writing: a million words honeycombed in my brain, each for its own perfected purpose, a clear glass bell. How many times have I sat and listened to someone drone on predictably when suddenly they utter a pearl? By God, my ear drums echo and my toes curl. A phrase like *I'm about as beat as the backside of a rug* or *The cat hedge-hopped up to the butter dish*. The blandest face blazes with imagination: a brain like no other, a private compartment on a flying train. There's no reason to be dusty-tongued with a rusty voicebox squeezing out squeaks. The world's aloft with all sorts of undiscovered similes and metaphors. Writing is an apple snapping its branch, a wave exploding, the swerve of a kiss …

Eastwood 1908

... I've come to realize that I'm an awful flirt, my
fingers darting in and out of every cat's cage. Will the
perfect woman, graceful as a breeze on the nape of my
neck, ever be able to forgive me? My dilemma is too
much imagination, serious spells of giddiness and
fever. I dwell in a kind of indigo cloud in a cosmos the
colour of dying violets. A glimpse of pale wrists and
ankles coaxes the sky to lean down in a blue mist.
These are not silly flirtations. I can't help myself. The
possibility of love makes me feel like a lonely God
destined or damned to live several feet off the ground. I
reach beyond myself, a sad blue light haloing the
distance. This is not a tease, but the voice of the future
crying, *I desire as far as I can see* ...

Croydon 1909

... after a life of teaching row upon row of inter-
changeable boys, my corpse would be propped up
against a blackboard, a textbook glued to stiff-clutched
hands. Not the life for me: confident, talented and mad
as I am. The educational system is primarily in place to
teach restrictions and rules; think six inches at a time,
conjugate your passions into a dozen harmless tenses,
memorize borders and don't overstep, dream poetry
that wouldn't offend a Sunday shoe. Small boys
splintered into smaller men, so the world spins, like
ants pushing a carousel. Is it arrogant that I will run
away and write the sort of books that stall machinery?
I must not mistake myself for brave, or other flatteries.
A writer isn't a special case. Just an ornery ant, or wait,
a cricket hatched by a family of black ants, an
impossible worker who can't help but chirp at the first
taste of dew, a singer of dark, grassy knells ...

Somewhere...
London 1910

From the cloudy bustle of Charing Cross
the stairs greet paradise in a
great tiger's-eye of electric
lights; where expectations unite.

Women with their perfumed waggeries
stream from silky stores. Bookshop
windows wink with expensive paper
while theatre marquees sweep down
across the streets like velvet capes.

On the edge of discovery
narrow lanes veering into frilly squares
zooming their way through
circuses and parks. Round every corner
another corner leading to eternity.

Mr. Hueffer breaks his literary bread
in the whirr of Trafalgar Square.
Critics crowd the Tower gates
and call gloriously for heads.
Oh, newsprint afternoons
the city castled in books.
Mr. Lawrence walks like a royal verb.

The perfect city is a swoon
done up in essences and trimmed
with metaphors. I am wobbling
in pleasure, my eyes thrilled wide.
The never-dared made drunk.

Somewhere on a haunted street
deadman Dickens writes impressions
in the energetic air. The sentence
carries on. Somewhere a white peacock
speaks its rarity to all sorts of men.
The deed is done, just waiting to be written.

London, halfway between the earth
and moon ... men like me trotting
on the light, trying to toss
reflections on an unsuspecting world.
Each silver street
rounding out the future.

Croydon *1911*

... I have written myself out with *Nethermere*†. Too windy and rhapsodic, as if the tablets handed to Moses turned out to be nothing but cloud. In fact, the whole outside world feels fog-heavy. This damn illness saps me and I stick to the sheets. Yet, a badly dressed blessing as well: the Dr. warns me I can't go back to teaching or I'll end up consumptive. So, I'm saved and tossed aside in the same blow. Free, but desperately frail; dropped, and barely holding on. I pray silently to those healthy men I pass on the streets that I might borrow a glow or two of them. My mind is as active as the sparks shooting up from Hell, but my body has been whittled down to soft white pulp ...

†the early title of *The White Peacock*

London 1912

... but when I strived to know Jessie, she acted out
everything I asked; love was a ragged attempt to please
rather than a passion. With Louie, love was always the
future, the present moment transformed into a
swallow trapped inside a cramped house. Ah, but this
Frieda I'm burning to write about, a most unlikely
woman, married to a nearly elderly professor, mother
of three children, the will of a mountain range. With
Frieda, love has been three steps forward and a naked
embrace. Now, flawed, forever. At our first meeting,
the French windows were flung open, the curtains
revealing the wind like the skirts of a shameless
goddess. The second time, Easter Sunday, the children
were racing about the garden in search of golden eggs.
Our third encounter, we walked in the woods and
sailed paper boats on a stream that led to the North
Sea. Why does all this sound so simpleminded and
symbolic? My tendency is to take life fast and too far, I
know this. But how else will life get anywhere, this
short, stubborn voyage. Frieda and I are meeting
tomorrow at Charing Cross, going away together, going
further than either of us have ever gone before ...

Italy 1914

… Frieda: she is much more than just a Mrs., spouse, consort, yoke-mate, affinity. Not even the most splendid of terms comes close enough to feel her breath against my cheek. She is, as the old Book insists, my missing rib, that ivory harp string to complete my grumbling concerto. But even more. She is the unreachable corner of my belly that has remained empty through whole flocks of dressy chickens and generous custards. She is the piercing, hairy eye in the back of my head. Ah, but more. She is the word ripping a canal in my tongue, the perfect sound of blood. She is the daughter of Baron von Richthofen, the dark half of my stiff upper lip. She is the freak miracle of an extra hand, a foot, a flaring nostril, thing after thing to set me apart. There is so damnably little of me to divide into two. She has multiplied my senses, my glands. She is the map my body follows, the burning chill at the seat of my spine, the yelp from my groin. She is flesh of the world, pores open wide, hankering, hungering …

Italy 1914 #2

... if only Europe could last forever, but Frieda misses her children and I am cut into pieces from lack of cash. Desperation nips at my not yet callous heels as I scamper back to Mother England, my tail wrapped around my neck like a hangman's noose. Ah, but there are finer words to write, finer memories. Yesterday, a picnic practically in the clouds, an eyeful of the Carrara mountains and the long, lean valley of the Magra. How the distant seacoast tucked itself around the tangled shore, such familiarity of elements, water and earth in perfect harmony. And the villages, like scattered pockets of gold dust, a fortune in noble, extraordinary lives. I almost made a running leap into the sparkling air; me bobbing over mountain peaks, my bare bottom eclipsing the sun. Better yet, I think I'll walk south, never stop walking, into the Apennines, into another dimension. Somewhere invisible where there aren't abandoned children and hollow bank accounts ...

... too much corruption, old age and a terror that sets man against man as if we were all gladiators. The English take to war with an uncommon fury, most of them not even caring to clarify the enemy. I am the enemy with my dirty little books and my abandoned patriotism. I am the enemy whenever I think a new thought. What I would most like to do is transform that newness into something greater than personality: a new spirit, a new life. Creativity, unanimity, rebirth. I will rush into the future and fix it from rolling down that endless hill of time. People don't understand that: reshaping the very essence of life, stopping God in his cold tracks. We have too long believed in weakness; if the Creator truly is, then his main ambition is to blow new life into his creations. Blow away! I have stopped stumbling and collapsing, I am breathing in ...

Omens…
Cornwall 1916

Waves climb the bony cliffs
a spray of silver-serpent light
dazzling on the meadow grass.
The ghosts of Cornwall's past
wear overcoats of mist
their inconsequential feet floating
inches above the endless mud
the dew drops clinging to
straw-coloured gorse, like frost.

Leaping over brambles
high-stepping grasps of ivy vines
I feel my English body
peel, my bones hollowing
into spokes or feathers. Only
the essence of a man can walk
on air; the rest of him
quickly drops and puddles.

Days pass where I hide
inside this stony cottage
shedding my skin on a rough
white page. A war is clutching
Europe, squeezing cities flat.
England trembles, damp and
ornery, searching the skies for
big black butterflies, pacing
the meadows bare. With poison pen
I end the lives of cowering
men, raising the blackberry
bushes to a wall of spikes.
There are soldiers tied tight
in the ivy, Germans and English alike.

I wait for the night when
a blessed bomb might split the shore
in two, when our little cottage
will float to sea complete with
garden and books. A new land then
an ideal ring of sparkling
waves, of roses tinged
with salt. Frieda and I will be
free of nationality
castaways like Adam and Eve.
To be an island is to be
complete, the whole world
recreated in a man.

Toss the gossips from their slick cliffs
let them cut the throats of sharks.
A critic or two bouncing on
a wave, nothing more than foam.
Let us roast the scavengers
and feed them to exotic birds.

For now though, all of England
is sharp and misshapen
a broken fist. Only the waves
are perky. Frieda and I dream
beyond accusations and black-outs
to a cracking time and place.
A severed hand slipping
from around our swollen necks.

I am an omen of life.
Look closely, I am an island
on the Cornish coast, a ghost
of what once was solid land.

Cornwall 1916

... what do I propose to do with the world? Sweep it all into one gloriously muddy pile of hothouse orchids and bamboo shoots, of kings and queens and porcelain Chinese dolls, of blood and pus, of thatched roofs and ivory towers, of porridge and ostrich eggs, of zippers and helium balloons, of snowy thighs and crimson bums, of *Childe Harold* and heroic couplets, of Goose Fair and Timbuktu, of coal dust and tsetse flies, all in one mountain of ooze. What then? I'll strike a measly match and poof! Isn't that what's meant when people say I want to set the world on fire? It's what I mean at any rate. A world come true in a column of smoke. The crimson ash of original man ...

Derby 1918

... the days before Christmas were as dreary as a cold hand in an empty pocket. How can people live whole lives this way, penny poor, timid of tomorrow, terrified that something might change for the worse? On the day before Christmas Eve, my sister and her family were hunched over, chilly, fretting several months ahead of themselves, the February sniffles, the April mud. But come actual, verifiable Christmas, spirits suddenly soared, stained glass butterflies bursting out of mousy cocoons. Food fit for a robust choir of angels: giant turkey, tongues, roast loin of pork, sausages, mince pies, almond tarts, cheesecakes, puddings, jellies, enough to soothe the blackest hearts. Then, in the evening, songs and boozy rhymes, and a game of charades that made most melodramas look like tissue paper. I'll never forget their faces: in the pink, all ablaze, a million miles away from a trace of anxiety. If I thought this would last, I'd put down the longest roots in the whole county and celebrate until my ancient bones turned to fluff. But just a day away faces fall again, tables are scrubbed clean and nightmares make their grimaces. I'm getting out of here, even if I have to stretch a pound twice as far as my legs can reach. Soon, Frieda and I will travel around the globe, perhaps settling in America where people have yet to surrender to tomorrow and tomorrow and tomorrow. To set ourselves apart from the world, is that so impossible? To live in each pure moment of joy or misery until that moment freely ends ...

Capri 1920

... on our way to the rest of the world. We arrived in Capri on a steamer no sturdier than a bathtub; a blood red dawn was just beginning to pour over the Mediterranean. I plan to enter Ceylon on the back of a swordfish, although Frieda would prefer a flying carpet complete with pillows and bowls of exotic fruit. As for Australia, I might just ride in on a tidal wave. And America, I think a bird would do nicely, a bald eagle with ruthless eyes. I can just picture Frieda ensconced on a pile of feathers, sailing a hundred feet above California. The image is completely sublime ...

Arabian Sea 1922

... the strangest feeling gliding down the Suez Canal, the eyes not missing a palm tree or a sand dune; no matter how foreign a landscape appears, the brain insistently recites every glimpse of solid earth. I am reminded that the physical world rules me: I am nothing more than bones and uncontrollable sensations. But out at sea, the feeling fades, the brain scrubbed clean. The land grows loose within me, dissolving, as if my muscles and thoughts are turning to salt water. I may not be able to walk by the time we arrive in Ceylon. My entire being will spill on the sun-baked docks, trickling back into the sea again. Either that or evaporating into thin air. It's the world and I at odds again; one of us will eventually disappear ...

Feeling the Heat ...
Ceylon 1922

May my eulogy advise that
once upon a time I survived
that scalding island known as
Ceylon. *In 1922*
the less-than-honourable
Mr. Lawrence almost died
from devilish heat, from shock.

Frieda shrugs both shoulders bare
her face protruding in the
snapping sun. *Pick me a coconut*
she sings. How the wife has a taste
for the poison in her husband's brain.
Her words take aim and flare.

I dream of her dancing over
steamy hills, the Lake of Kandy
coarse in the distance. A dance of
tea and cinnamon, of pealed
temple bells. Naked as
a Buddha, a real bellyful.

She dances night and day, six weeks
of footsteps in my memory.
These tropics are a selfish place:
stoking women into sparks
burying their men beneath
boiling rubber. Where loneliness sweats.

In my last dream Frieda is
a rather large flower, lazy
scarlet with petals loose as
tongues. And I, a worker bee
drowning in hot nectar
a final, choking buzz.

May Ceylon mistake the ocean
for a flower (and bending
to the scent, sink amidst
the scarlet waves). I am taking
Frieda out of dreams, my fist rising
on a cool pen. Passion
is better made than endured.

Australia 1922

... the smells of Ceylon clung to my nostril walls like iodine; a sickening image, but apt. The whole time I felt as if my membranes were dissolving, turning to mush. Only the nights kept me sane, a cool envelope of spices and funeral flowers, the world's end. What a contrast to be in Australia, a country without a distinct impression, like Dracula casting no reflection in a mirror. Here, expectations dwindle into half-forgotten shopping lists; there doesn't seem to be much reason for being at all. If Australia were a man, he'd be socially inept, massively built and empty-eyed, without a clear purpose or a determining lust. All vacant body, a handsome house hollow to the chimney. Soul or spirit is the missing link, a deep animation that just doesn't exist. Yet, I don't mean to imply misery, only absence. Like kissing one of those swell-looking mannequins: interesting, but it won't kiss back, no matter what ...

From the Kangaroo Tree…
Australia 1922

From the kangaroo tree, Aboriginal
(original) man surveys his promised
land. Koala bears beam
from the turquoise surf.

I close my eyes and wish to be
a smidgen of the eucalyptus shore.

Enwreathe me in Australian hope.
Once upon a time
the world began again.

In our pretty coastal cottage
near the civil market town
I feel as if the globe
had fallen upside down
ruining/rearranging the shape
of everything. As if heaven
had dropped like a meteor.
There are rocks and sea, plenty of
dazed sheep, and people
chatting up the postman
for news only half-a-mile away.
Where are the leaping trees, the
tame bears? Oh, second-hand dreams.

Close your eyes for just an instant
and the world will end.

More and more of me is living
on an island. Stunning
scenery. Men and women, unbroken
promises. A love of flesh
an overwhelming thankfulness.
Beyond Australia? I cannot see ...
the world keeps getting in the way.

San Francisco 1922

... twenty-five days at sea have transformed my legs into a skinny pair of fins and my imagination into an incredible aquarium. I have no stamina for San Francisco with its hard ground and substantial Palace Hotel. I collapse into a creamy white bathtub and hallucinate silver dolphins peering over windowsills. But I am still ecstatic in the midst of my instability. I have rediscovered land! The perfect world contains a blue bedspread, fresh eggs, streetlamps and a glorious array of steep, unexplored hills. *I am a man*, I whisper to myself and so far no-one has hissed back, *No, you're not, you're an Englishman*. I'm a man and a fish together, Virgo earth and crashing waves. I can almost feel the future: slippery yet solid, like the bottom of the sea ...

Possibilities...
America 1923

Strange, the Americans graft
themselves to crowded towns
generic cities. Glass eyes
afraid of shattering. They are
clinging to spring avenues
hugging creamy walls, pushing
outskirts further out. Pretending
the land no longer exists.

A land where people can
surrender to the blood, the
feuding seasons, where life basks
upon prehistoric rocks
rejoicing over opals of
sweat, flamingo feathers, flesh
reshaped by a squeeze of
August wind. America
sneaks itself on the world
like a treasure map. A land where
blood streams from the Rockies, splashing
over canyons and meadows
staining both the desert and
the sea with a suicidal
sunset; a land dying from
the sheer beauty of its
possibilities.

Summer faints amongst the holy pines.
Winter binds the valleys
in a grip of empty ice. And
through it all, abundant eyes: a field
of quartz, a million apple trees
a finger painting of
the Northern Lights. America
makes me sweat in its Everglades
take flight from its bleached abandoned
bones, breathe to the roar of
a waterfall. America
insists on surrender
bleeding me of normal vision.

The Painted Life ...
New Mexico 1923

At sunset: Frieda solid on a black mare
a corsage of yucca blossoms
tucked in her dress. Looks like
the moon is rising from her breasts.
Love resurrected in the light.

When I paint this desert I am painting
my own footprints surrounded by
a sea of sand. Frieda sits
on a black island, bucking valiantly
through the dry waves. We are alone
horizons dropping with the sun
like walls of a grave.

The black mare grows edgy;
night is nowhere for the beast
following its sight. Frieda dismounts
eclipsed by the great flanks of
her island. When the self disappears
darkness simply fills the narrow space.

Until the last I shall grovel
for the merest light. Painting after
painting of tumbled sun, of a transparent
life. And when finally dark
bury me in the valley of Frieda's breasts
so thoughts of me will seem to rise
with the slightest of breaths.

Oaxaca, Mexico 1924

... I was drawn south by mythology: the blazing, vast, inhuman, uncivilized voices of the gods. I mistook Mexico for a walking, talking spiritual life, a land where the rivers ran with scalding blood and the deserts bloomed tiny pink angels that, from a distance, looked a lot like phalluses. Could I have been going mad, dreaming up this netherworld? Frieda's palm against my forehead smells of black toast. I must hold on to what reality I can obtain: this lost, mountainous town, lost between the Pacific and the Atlantic like a toppled fence, a trampled boundary, home of starved socialism and Indians in vests and suspenders, of dead gods and dreams of Mexico City a lifetime away. The only mythology left in this world within a world is a new railroad line, a quarter-finished road, a six-month-old newspaper from Madrid. What can I hope will sustain me? I feel like I'm slowly backing out of Eden, my footprints on fire ...

Del Monte Ranch, Questa, New Mexico 1924

... here where I first really noted how darkness doesn't
fall at all, but devours. Like a cold mouth calling low
from the clouds: this is the moment the world will
end. It consumes our weakling faith, gobbles down our
flickering eyes, licks us up as if we were tiny puddles.
Frieda always slips inside the cabin just as the sun is
about to be sucked from the sky, while I walk out to
where the alfalfa field will be swallowed and watch as
the darkness feeds on the hills. The pines and the firs
are the first to go black. Then the aspens and
cottonwoods: trees ten times my size gulped in a flash.
The scrub-oaks seem to bleed before they disappear,
bloodstains on the rocks. And then it comes for me,
my feet tangled in the grass. Deliriously, I want to run,
bound over those last sips of light. But I close my eyes,
remain, solid as any tree, knowing that when I look
again, the darkness will be everything, everywhere, and
I no more than an alfalfa seed stuck between cold
teeth. It's strangely peaceful to be so much a part of a
demolished world. I feel my blind way back to Frieda,
blending in with her invisibly ...

Chasing Your Shadow...
Mexico 1925

In the baked streets, parades of
children hiss like dragons.
They are chasing the devil
into a hot peacock sea.

I wait for innocence to
return, this bed of beaded death
this hideous heat. Each breath
a half-lit foyer where
life lurks watching for sunny clouds
of dust, for children beaming
through small, dirty hands.

The child Montezuma
chased his death to a gleam of wealth.
Tiny sapphires teasing
on a wave's tongue: the souls of
banished Aztecs, long ago
mistaken for evil eyes.
In Mexico you are either
dead or pushing death away
chasing your own shadow
across hard red clay.

Call it inflammation
consumption, chagrin.
My own death feels like
the death of a civilization.
The child Bertie chases Lorenzo
to the edge of the burnt-out bed.

Del Monte Ranch, Questa, New Mexico 1925

... breathing in a nip of evening air, moonlight cools
my lungs; I breathe out the tiniest crystals of oxygen,
like those stars on the tips of fairy tale wands. Malaria,
'flu, tropical fever and an assortment of other demons, I
almost died, a string of breath being pulled out of a
hole in my chest, I couldn't find the daylight, not even
in the sun. I'm back here now ten weeks, close to
strong again, feeling strangely at peace. There is no
paradise, but if there was, I'd set it down beneath this
pine tree, this moonlit chair. Let Frieda scream for me,
books holler, food tantalize, I won't budge an inch. I've
been looking for the perfect world my entire life,
sorting through air and moonbeams, through demons
and death. All the while it was here, just this moment,
almost satisfied ...

Del Monte Ranch, Questa, New Mexico 1925 #2

… during the past few weeks I've coaxed a stream of
water down from Gallina Canyon to irrigate the fields;
coaxed is a literary word, meaning digging, hauling
rocks, sweating like kettles. Every morning and
evening I milk our huge black cow whose only purpose
in life is to one day kick me squarely between the eyes.
Frieda is driven wild by our eleven hens whom she
swears are trying to crush their own eggs just to
deprive us of nourishment. This is an absurdly savage
life, no grace for a writer. Frieda has talked me into
Europe by autumn, somewhere warm, of course. When
you don't believe in kingdom come, you settle for a
soft alternative, a great, bouncy bed of a land where
you can put your feet up and watch the past sail by …

Afterlife...
the Atlantic Ocean 1925

Have you seen the way caterpillars
curl themselves in leaves?
So the ship rolls beneath wave after
wave. Wrapped in water, incomplete
our hands and feet disintegrate.
Splashily the afterlife unfolds.

Heaven is a coral reef where God
sits gingerly. Could that be the devil
stirring up the depthless muck?
Swim or fly, the eternal muscles
are the same. To spend what's left of me
afloat. A bitter salty spray.

The Christmas Eve Abyss...
Florence 1927

The abyss is, contrary to
empty minds, full-up. High
Anglicans, springer spaniels
packets of liver and
brotherly love. The Prince of
Darkness is a wet Londoner
up to his loins in mud.

Frieda decorates our gnarled
Italian Christmas tree. Seashells
nuzzling in the branches
to remind me of the great blue
world beyond. Candles to
enlighten. Good German
that she is, Frieda pantomimes
a paradise. Insistent self.

I should like to take root here
in Florence. Firenze: where
Dante ogled the crowds of hell
where DaVinci raised an empty
gaze to God. In art, death
is a way of seeing things.

Tonight, Christ's eve, heaven
is a sympathetic act.
The western world sets fire
to its trees and everyone
believes the abyss is but
a wisp of pallid smoke.

Gstaad 1928

... yet another cold, my hands actually trembling and
the fever digging deep inside. Too many weather
changes here: one day the pigeons are basking in the
square, the next I'm being blown into buildings. It's a
wonder I stay alive. I'm thinging more and more of
New Mexico, how I let myself be talked into running
away. Frieda's unhappiness, the children, her family,
the old scars. I had no choice but to try and believe the
new world was dead. But Europe is the true corpse, a
stony rigor mortis, a putrid culture of crumbling
picture galleries and wormy mortality. The men I meet
in the streets all have strained eyes, inscribed with
family trees that look like burst veins. And the
womens' mouths have been surgically frozen into
gasps of horror, horror at a glimpse of desire or a fresh
blue breeze. It's no surprise that my *John Thomas*† has
met with such raging disgust. European civilization
was long ago severed at the waist (imagine a burial
ground brimming over with loins and butts and wilted
genitalia) and dropped upon a marble horse. *Oh, look
at the lovely statue*, the tourists say, devouring every
sexless, crippled inch ...

†an early title for *Lady Chatterley's Lover*

Mallorca 1929

... pride is where the Spanish are stuck, like colourful little insects preserved in amber: a sight to be seen, but a dead sight after all. Still, I abandon myself to the dizzy smell of orange blossoms and the great nude sun. My health is as bad as expected. I am two men in one: a new breed of adventurer on the brink of a discovery far greater than Columbus and his mortal America and, at the exact same time, a broken heart and a shrivelled spirit on the verge of extinction. I would like to trust totally in heaven, the world pared to one exposed nerve, yet the immediate future feels like a smokestack feeding me each and every breath. As always though, I'm not surrendering to a bloody thing. If I have to carry a dead body around with me for the rest of my life, so be it. Whenever I close my eyes, I can still see the outline of a perfect world: an island off the coast of possibility ...

Breathless ...
the Sanatorium 1930

Doubting Thomas lies abed
no longer believing in
breath. The lungs have no loyalty –
soggy, fair-weather friends.

Such a grave faux pas: misplacing
hope. Somewhere on the mountainside
a lucky coin dived from my
pocket. My rabbit's foot hopped away
like the cripple it always was.
Now for the blundering truth.

Breath is a habit, tearing away.
I was propelled through the world
by the force of my heartiest dreams.
Accustomed to the come and go
of desire. *What is the grand*
man made of? Nothing but the day
to day. Without
the predictable body
there are no higher schemes.

I am the air in the child's
balloon, a slow leak.

Life the mellifluous.
Chrysanthemums panting pink.
Women gulping kisses. Serpents
shedding lives. I am exhaled
by the night with its memories
of moths and comets, by
mimosas trembling in a prickly breeze.

Doubting Thomas gasps for a reason
not to die. Gasps for the
invisible, the impossible proof.

Last Lights...
Vence 1930

These days the sun is carted in
from a stagnant horizon
Aldous and Maria lifting
alongside the peasants; with
raised arms they urge the light against
my window, making me want to
believe the sky has stumbled
almost into my hands.

I am always competent to
see – my eyes, such blazing
windowframes. Though my ankles
hesitate, though my heart hides
beneath a tomb of ribs, though my
head is shovel-heavy, I
insist to see: these walls as white
as virgins, that orange cat leaping
into Frieda's multicoloured
lap, those books gleaming
like underwater rocks
on the table a lifetime away.
Look at the blue vase, the
purple flowers: a bruise
arranged in a glimmer.

Strange how I – blood and earth and
thumbs – have become colourless
a piece of timid crystal
glaring down from a mantel.
In this kindly light I am weak
with rainbows. On Frieda's lips
I am something deep and pink.
Next to a pot of ink I am
a robin's egg. Only in the dark
am I dull and watery
the colour of a window
with the shade drawn fully down.

No energy to save this
savage world. Black deserts will
remain heartless. Grey men
simply stay grey. To be
happy now is to watch a tanned
boy change the shape of the sea.
Even the cat with its silly
bits of string, its dreams of
embraceable birds, has too much
purpose for me. I watch
a corner of the bed vanish
in the blinding yellow noon.

Each breath as long as a year.
The world lengthens into evenings.
My feet seem far away.

Vence, pretty villa.
Frieda looks to the south, nothing
but the edges of waves. Yet
another day outlasted, the
sun buried in fields of clouds.

Who presses the moon against
my window? Something oozing from
a rotten sky. Huxley, words are
finally beyond us.
Maria, pages are falling
on my eyes. In the rocking chair
Frieda knits the horrid white pus
the orange cat dangling from her lap.

A Million Words ...
Vence 1930

Seasons are arranged in a vase
by the window: a veil of violets
dusty daisies, a wrinkled-yellow
chestnut spray. Icicles grow clear
and thin, like magic flutes.

Phosphorus looks down upon us all
a crystal God who knows the shape of
marrow in our bones. Wind is to snap
us, rain to wilt. Sunlight needles.
Fingers digging fast, the ends of
earth, the glowing rock of graves.

What I will miss most about the world
is change. Introspective skies
suddenly catching sight of closed
umbrellas. Real flesh and blood
emerging from the sombre cells of
books. Women revealing their unexpected
selves. Someone else's death.

From this dying hand came the brandishing
of clouds and torches: a dream landscape
where meadows flourished under crops of
birds, spreading into continental shelves.
The birth of an ideal sustains the man
until both become a way of life; death
diminishing nothing but the self.

Years from here a stranger will walk
into my house, *the home of the infamous*
etc ..., claiming to feel my spirit
in the antique walls. Only the words
always wanting out.

The world of the dead is a megalopolis.
Shakespeare scrunched beside Wordsworth
who I could swear is almost sitting
on my knee. The combination of us all
will haunt you, the quantity.

I rush too far ahead, the daily world
peeling from my brain like cobweb.
All I seem to care about is living
not the life itself. The taste of water
rather than the soggy map. The sound
of words, touch of body hair, smell of
sea, look of mirrors. I will leave
nothing of myself behind, just these
second-hand sensations never quite complete.

The world is eternal, not the man.
I was something in the air, in the
rosebush: a spot of cold, a thorn.

Field upon field of daisies. Chestnuts
falling like a skyful of wish-wearied
stars. The countryside unconscious
with snow. The world is larger than
an eye or mouth, and death promises
to be fuller than even the greediest of
hands. I do not believe in puny ghosts
but in giant plans: a lifetime that
just might change the way the world
goes on alone.

When I Close My Eyes ...
Vence, March 1930

Death is tiresomely emphatic
chanting to the listless brain
like a demon trained in an army
camp. *Die, die,* the syllable
storms my bed; sleep standing guard
a blindfold and a pair of heavy
hands. Let me go as purposefully
as Christ upon his sparkling cross.
A knife slicing light into keepsakes
of gold. But death is a held-back
breath, a total brute: memories
turning black and blue. Just
another shadow in a velvet box
another absence. How can one love
the world's nonchalance? Neither
island nor summit can save me now.
Life speeds through the valleys.
Watch closely, the wind on solid rock.

Somewhere in time, Frieda placed
her light on my windowsill
where a lifetime of sun
sucked it pale and dry.
In the future, an orange cat
sits licking its skeleton.
The world I know unravels
to a cold click of needles.

Losing track. Death, the muddled
chariot, looks more like a rocking
chair. I want to fight
but not to care.

The last light is definitely
yellow, but shallow as a fingerprint.
Easy to slip or skim. A
passing thought.

When I close my eyes
my hands completely disappear.

Books Are

Books do not breathe, or
share your soup, stroke your
arms, inhale your rare perfumes.
Books do not spit, love or scheme
for more. Books do not live
parallel lives. Books do not
pray or hold mirrors unto God.
Books do not die with regrets.

What books do is talk
endlessly. Not to you or
the sycamores or the china
cups, but to no avail at all.
Talk, more talk. Books have
something to say and are bound
to say it. Books equal
their words exactly.

Since my last letter I have
been a book or several books
together. I do not listen
or spit. I talk to thin air.

Books are and emphasize.
Nothing, they chant and storm
will ever stay the same. The
wind on everything, pages
turned, pages torn.

Acknowledgements:

Some of these poems have appeared in the following publications: *Arc, Canadian Literature, The Fiddlehead, Grain, The New Quarterly, Prairie Fire, The Prairie Journal of Canadian Literature, Prism, Quarry, Queen's Quarterly & Zymergy.* I am grateful to the editors for their encouragement.

For biographical information and atmosphere, I am indebted to the Cambridge edition of *The Letters of D.H. Lawrence,* Harry T. Moore's *The Priest of Love, a Life of D.H. Lawrence* (Penguin) and Anthony Burgess' *Flame into Being, the Life and Work of D.H. Lawrence* (Stoddart).

Special thanks to Karen Ruttan and Don McKay for their excellent editorial advice, and to Brian Vanderlip, Isabelle Saunders, Stephen Morrissey, Sonja Skarstedt, Allan Brown and Robert Hilles for their inspiring words.

About the Author

Letters from a Long Illness with the World is Barry Dempster's fifth volume of poetry. He has also published two collections of short stories and a children's novel, and he is the poetry and reviews editor of *Poetry Canada Review*.

KEN BATIUK